Letterland

My name is

_____

Let's learn about...

ch   sh   h   th   wh   ph

a_e   ai   ay   e_e   ee   ea   y

i_e   ie   igh   y   o_e   oa   ow

Level 2 - Workbook 1

Draw lines from Clever Cat and Harry Hat Man to the things that start with their sound. Circle the one that doesn't.

Draw something that starts with the '**ch**' sound.

Draw a line around the '**ch**' words in the grid below. They go across and down.

c	h	i	c	k	e	n
h	s	c	l	c	a	c
a	c	h	e	e	s	e
i	x	o	h	w	n	o
r	j	p	c	h	i	n
p	e	a	c	h	e	s

chair

chicken

peaches

cheese

chop

Can you find one more '**ch**' word in the grid? Copy it on to the lines.

____ ____ ____ ____

3

Write '**ch**' on the lines to complete these words.

 _____ in

 _____ air

 _____ icken

 pea _____ es

 _____ ildren

Draw lines from Sammy Snake and Harry Hat Man to the things that start with their sound. Circle the one that doesn't.

Draw something that starts with a '**sh**' sound.

Write '**sh**' on the lines to complete these words.

 _____ op

 _____ oe

 _____ ell

 _____ ip

 fi _____

Choose the correct sound to start the pictures below. Write the letters on the lines.

shop   chop

_____ op

ship   chip

_____ ip

shin   chin

in

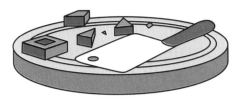

shop   chop

op

Draw lines from Talking Tess and Harry Hat Man to the things that include their sound. Circle the one that doesn't.

Draw something that starts with a '**th**' sound.

Write '**th**' on the lines to complete these words.

3 ____ree

 ____row

 ____ank you

 pa____

 ba____

Fill in the missing letters **sh**, **ch** or **th** to complete the sentences below. Read the sentences out loud.

This is a fi____.

This is a ____ip.

This man ____ops logs on ____e pa____.

Can you hear Tess and Harry whispering or saying their sound? Copy the words below on to the lines in the correct box.

three   that   this   thin

thanks

_____

_____

those

_____

_____

Find the objects starting with Walter Walrus and Harry Hat Man's sound. Tick a box as you find each one then rainbow write the letter shapes.

whale

wheat

whistle

Draw lines from Walter Walrus and Harry Hat Man to the things that include their sound.
Circle the one that doesn't.

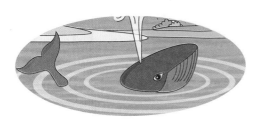

Draw something that starts with a '**wh**' sound.

Can you hear Walter or Harry saying their sound? Copy the words below on to the lines in the correct box.

whisk   **whose**   **why**   **whole**

when

_____

_____

who

_____

_____

Find the objects starting with Peter Puppy and Harry Hat Man's sound. Tick a box as you find each one then rainbow write the letter shapes.

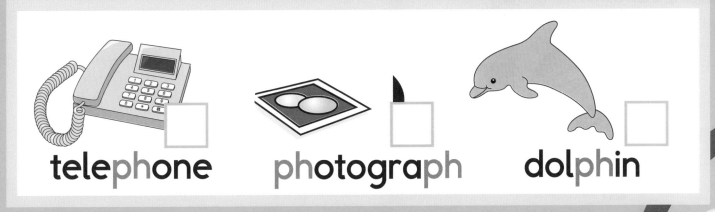

telephone   photograph   dolphin

Draw lines from Peter Puppy and Harry Hat Man to the things that include their sound.
Circle the one that doesn't.

3

Draw something that starts with a '**ph**' sound.

Draw a line around the '**ph**' and '**wh**' words in the grid below. They go across and down.

p	h	i	z	k	e	w
h	w	h	a	l	e	h
w	h	i	s	t	l	e
i	x	o	h	w	n	a
p	h	o	n	e	i	t
h	p	h	o	t	o	g

whistle

wheat

phone

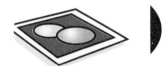

photo

Can you find one more '**wh**' word in the grid? Copy it on to the lines.

_____ _____ _____ _____

Read the sentences and put your stickers in the correct places to complete the picture.

1. Put a chick on the path.

2. Put a chick on the bath.

3. Put a fish in the shop.

4. Put three shells in the path.

Listen →

Listen to the words.
Put a tick next to the sound you hear.

Track 24

At the start

1. **ch** ☐   **sh** ☐    **th** ☐   **ph** ☐   **wh** ☐

2. **ch** ☐   **sh** ☐    **th** ☐    **ph** ☐    **wh** ☐

3.  **ch** ☐   **sh** ☐    **th** ☐    **ph** ☐    **wh** ☐

At the end

1. **ch** ☐   **sh** ☐   **th** ☐

2. **ch** ☐   **sh** ☐   **th** ☐

Listen again This exercise requires careful listening skills.
Listen more than once if you need to.

Listen Listen to the words and put a tick next to the one you hear. The first one has been done for you.

Track 25

1. ✓  ☐  ☐

2.  ☐  ☐  ☐

3.  ☐  ☐  ☐

4.  ☐ 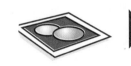 ☐  ☐

5.  ☐  ☐ 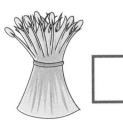 ☐

Listen again — This exercise requires careful listening skills. Listen more than once if you need to.

Can you hear Mr A in these words? Circle the object in which you can't hear Mr A saying his name.

Think of an '**a_e**' word and draw it.

Circle the '**a_e**' word that rhymes in each row.

lake

cat

snake

ant

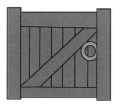

gate

hat

bat

skate

rake

ink

cake

sack

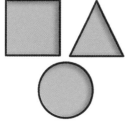

shapes

grapes

ship

shop

Draw a line around the '**a_e**' words in the grid below. They go across and down.

o	n	s	k	a	t	e
b	x	p	e	i	z	p
g	r	a	p	e	s	c
a	s	d	w	g	h	a
t	v	e	b	u	o	k
e	o	y	l	a	k	e

spade

cake

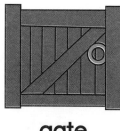

gate

grapes

lake

Can you find one more '**a_e**' word in the grid? Copy it on to the lines.

___ ___ ___ ___ ___

Draw lines from Mr A and Mr I to the things that include them out walking. Circle the one that doesn't.

Think of an '**ai**' word and draw it.

Draw lines to join each picture with the correct word.

chain

train

rain

nail

snail

paint

Write '**ai**' on the lines to complete these words.

r __ __ n

sn __ __ l

tr __ __ n

p __ __ nt

ch __ __ n

Draw lines from Mr A and Yellow Yo-yo Man to the things that include them out walking. Circle the one that doesn't.

Think of an '**ay**' word and draw it.

Mr A and Yellow Yo-yo Man are going on holiday. Circle all the '**ay**' words on their postcard.

Friday 9th May

Today we ate a takeaway!

To

_____
Write your name on the line.

What did Mr A and Yellow Yo-yo Man eat today?
Colour the correct picture.

cake

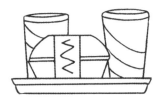

takeaway

apple

Mr A and Yellow Yo-yo Man like to go out walking at the end of every day. Write them on the lines to finish the days.

Mond_____   Tuesd_____

Wednesd_____

Thursd_____   Frid_____

Saturd_____   Sund_____

What day is it today? Copy the correct day onto the line.

_____

Fill in the missing letters to complete the sentences below. Then listen and repeat the sentences.

They h___t___ the r___n.

The p___nt is in the tr___.

It's a birthd___ c___k___.

It's R___c___ D___,
tod___.

New words

Make the individual sounds. Then start to blend the sounds to make and learn some new words.

 cave

 wave

Sticker time

Read the sentences and put your stickers in the correct places to complete the picture.

Put a snail on the cake.

Put a snail on the hay.

Put a cake in front of the train.

Put a nail on the path.

Listen Listen to the words. Put a tick next to the correct spelling pattern. The first one has been done for you.

Track 40

How do you spell it?

1.  ✓  ☐ ☐

2.  ☐  ☐ ☐

3.  ☐  ☐ ☐

4.  ☐  ☐ ☐

5.  ☐  ☐  ☐

Listen again This exercise requires careful listening skills. Listen more than once if you need to.

Listen  Listen to the words and put a tick next to the one you hear. The first one has been done for you.

 Track 41

1.  ✓

2.

3.

4.

5.

Listen again

This exercise requires careful listening skills.
Listen more than once if you need to.

35

Can you hear Mr E in these words? Circle the object in which you can't hear Mr E saying his name.

Think of an '**e_e**' word and draw it.

Draw a cross through the green letters to delete them. Write the red letters on the lines to make an '**e_e**' word.

Which '**e_e**' word have you made?

_____ _____ _____ _____ _____ _____

Write '**e_e**' on the lines to complete these words.

athl__t__

del__t__

sc__n__

comp__t__

St__v__

Draw lines from Mr E and his brother to the things that include them out walking. Circle the one that doesn't.

Think of an '**ee**' word and draw it.

Circle the '**ee**' word that rhymes in each row.

 **three**

 **sweet**

 **tree**

 train

 **sweep**

 **jet**

 **zip**

 **jeep**

 **queen**

 green

 **hen**

 **quilt**

 **cheese**

 **hat**

 **chop**

 **sneeze**

Draw a line around the '**ee**' words in the grid below. They go across and down.

s	l	e	e	p	a	s
l	f	z	g	t	w	w
j	e	o	k	r	z	e
j	e	e	p	e	v	e
p	t	h	l	e	d	p
c	h	e	e	s	e	k

sweep

sleep

jeep

cheese

tree

Can you find one more '**ee**' word in the grid? Copy it on to the lines.

___ ___ ___ ___

Draw lines from Mr E and Mr A to the things that include them out walking. Circle the one that doesn't.

Think of an '**ea**' word and draw it.

Write 'ee' or 'ea' on the lines to complete these words.

ee   ea

l   f

ee   ea

tr

ee   ea

j   p

ee   ea

p   s

Read the sentences and add to the pictures to match.

A leaf on a peach.

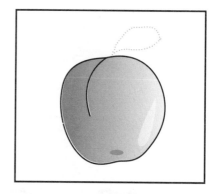

A seal on a beach.

A pea on a snail.

A cup of tea.

Look for the words where Yellow Yo-yo Man helps Mr E. Tick a box as you find each one then rainbow write the letter shape.

family

party

puppy

Draw lines from Yellow Yo-yo Man to the things that include him saying his new sound for Mr E. Circle the thing that doesn't.

Think of a 'y' word and draw it.

Draw a line around the '**y**' words in the grid below. They go across and down.

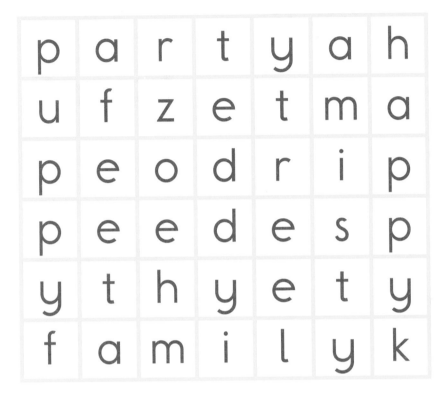

p	a	r	t	y	a	h
u	f	z	e	t	m	a
p	e	o	d	r	i	p
p	e	e	d	e	s	p
y	t	h	y	e	t	y
f	a	m	i	l	y	k

misty

family

party

puppy

teddy

Can you find one more
'**y**' word in the grid?
Copy it on to the lines.

___ ___ ___ ___ ___

Fill in the missing letters to complete the sentences below. Then listen and repeat the sentences.

The qu___n likes to be cl___n.

It's not ___sy sw___ping l___ves.

Mr E del___t__s the tr___.

Let's ___t cr___m cakes with t___.

Use your stickers to label the picture below. Look back in your book if you need help remembering the spellings.

Write down one more word you can see in the picture that has an e_e, ee, ea or y sound. _____

Listen

 Listen to the words. Put a tick next to the correct spelling pattern. The first one has been done for you.

 Track 60

How do you spell it?

1.  ☑    ☐    ☐

2.  ☐     ☐    ☐

3.  ☐    ☐    ☐

4.  ☐    ☐    ☐

5.  ☐    ☐    ☐

50

Listen again

This exercise requires careful listening skills. Listen more than once if you need to.

Listen

Listen to the words and put a tick next to the one you hear. The first one has been done for you.

Track 61

1.

2.

3.

4.

5.

Listen again

This exercise requires careful listening skills.
Listen more than once if you need to.

51

Can you hear Mr I in these words? Circle the object where you can't hear Mr I saying his name.

5

Think of an 'i_e' word and draw it.

Five and nine are
both 'i_e' words.

How many slides can you count?

Draw more kites so that there are five altogether.

Count nine limes and colour them.

Write '**i_e**' on the lines to complete these words.

b __ k __

m __ c __

sl __ d __

k __ t __

l __ m __

Find the objects that include Mr I and Mr E out walking. Tick a box as you find each one then rainbow write the letter shapes.

tie ☐   pie ☐   flies ☐

Draw lines from Mr I and Mr E to the things that include them out walking. Circle the one that doesn't.

Think of an '**ie**' word and draw it.

Mr I and Mr E like eating pies. Put a tick by all the things you could put in a pie for Mr I and Mr E. Circle the odd one out.

Draw a picture of something you'd like in a pie.

Draw lines from Mr I, Golden Girl and Harry Hat Man to the things that include them. Circle the one that doesn't.

Think of an '**igh**' word and draw it.

Draw a line around the '**igh**' words in the grid below. They go across and down.

l	a	v	g	f	s	e
i	y	z	h	i	j	o
g	w	r	i	g	h	t
h	e	q	g	h	b	o
t	d	b	h	t	k	c
u	n	i	g	h	t	c

light

right

night

fight

Can you find one more '**igh**' word in the grid? Copy it on to the lines.

___ ___ ___ ___

Write '**igh**' on the lines to complete these words.

l ____ t

r ____ t

n ____ t

f ____ t

Draw lines from Yellow Yo-yo Man to the things that include him saying his new sound for Mr I.

Think of a '**y**' word and draw it.

Write '**ie**' or '**y**' on the line to complete these words.

ie   y

sk _____

ie   y

p _____

ie   y

t _____

ie   y

cr _____

Write '**y**' on the lines to complete these words. Then match them to the pictures.

fl<u>y</u>

sk___

cr___

Jul___

wh___

Listen Fill in the missing letters to complete the sentences below. Then listen and repeat the sentences.

Track 79

Nick is n＿n＿,
ton＿＿＿t.

Kicking King can
f＿＿a k t＿.

He l＿k＿s p＿＿s.

He l＿k＿s sl＿d＿s.

Use your stickers to label the picture below. Look back in your book if you need help remembering the spellings.

Write down one more word you can see in the picture that has an i_e, ie, igh or y sound. _____

How do you spell it?

1.  ✓  ☐  ☐

2.  ☐  ☐  ☐

3.  ☐  ☐  ☐

4.  ☐  ☐  ☐

5.  ☐  ☐  ☐

4 spellings: 1 sound This exercise requires very careful listening skills. Listen at least three times before trying to complete it.

Listen

Listen to the words and put a tick next to the one you hear. The first one has been done for you.

Track 81

Listen again

This exercise requires careful listening skills.
Listen more than once if you need to.

Can you hear Mr O in these words? Circle the object in which you can't hear Mr O saying his name.

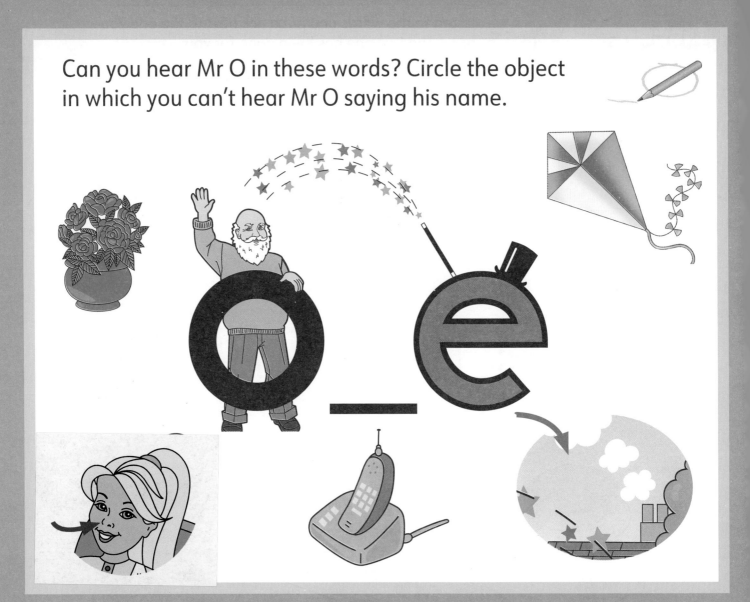

Think of an '**o_e**' word and draw it.

Circle the 'o_e' word that rhymes in each row.

phone

bone

pie

queen

nose

nail

rose

nine

rope

cup

envelope

jeep

robe

robot

red

globe

rope

nose

rose

phone

robe

smoke

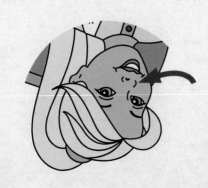

Find the words that include Mr O and Mr A out walking. Tick a box as you find each one then rainbow write the letter shapes.

goat

road

soap

Draw lines from Mr O and Mr A to the things that include them out walking. Circle the one that doesn't.

Think of an '**oa**' word and draw it.

Draw a line around the '**oa**' words in the grid below. They go across and down.

h	a	z	c	d	u	r
p	m	g	o	a	l	o
y	b	d	a	v	b	a
g	o	a	t	s	f	d
e	a	i	k	o	e	a
i	t	n	s	o	a	p

coat

goat

road

boat

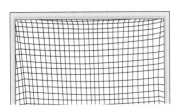

goal

Can you find one more
'**oa**' word in the grid?
Copy it on to the lines.

___ ___ ___ ___

Draw lines from Mr O and Walter Walrus to the things that include them. Circle the one that doesn't.

Think of an '**ow**' word and draw it.

Write '**ow**' on the lines to complete these words.
Then match them to the pictures.

sn____

b____l

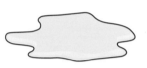

yell____

wind____

gr____

Write '**oa**' or '**ow**' on the lines to complete these words.

oa   ow

c ___ t

oa   ow

sn ___

oa   ow

r ___ d

oa   ow

b ___ l

Use your stickers to label the picture below. Look back in your book if you need help remembering the spellings.

The colour

COAST ROAD

Write down one more word you can see in the picture that has an **o_e**, **oa** or **ow** sound.

_____

Listen ➡

Fill in the missing letters to complete the sentences below. Then listen and repeat the sentences.

Track 95

This is a sl____b____t.

Sn____ is on the r____d.

Just a quick note.

note   envelope

Nick can see no n__t__ in the envel__p__.

How do you spell it?

1.  ✓  ☐  ☐

2.  ☐  ☐  ☐

3.  ☐  ☐  ☐

4.  ☐  ☐  ☐

5.  ☐  ☐  ☐

Listen

Listen to the words and put a tick next to the one you hear. The first one has been done for you.

Track 97

1.  ☐    ☐    ✓

2.  ☐    ☐    ☐

3.  ☐    ☐    ☐

4.  ☐    ☐    ☐

5.  ☐    ☐    ☐

Congratulations! You're ready for Level 2, Workbook 2.